Computer BASICS

BOOK 6

Jill Jesson

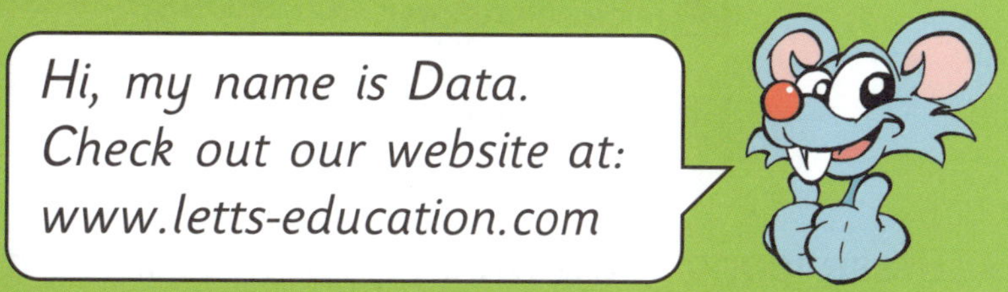

Contents

This book has been written for use with Microsoft Office 2000. The ideas suggested will also work well, with a few minor amendments, using many other programs including Microsoft Works, ClarisWorks, and AppleWorks on Apple machines. (see inside back cover for more details).

Young children may need help to start, save and print their work.

The first time your child uses this book you may need to help them learn each new skill. They will soon be able to practise by themselves.

To start

- Click on Start. Go up to Programs.
- Select one of the Microsoft Office icons.

From the Programs menu you can

- Click on
  - Microsoft Word — Word Processor
  - Microsoft Access — Database
  - Microsoft Excel — Spreadsheet

- These icons show which type of document you need. They appear immediately before the title of each page.

WP	Word Processing	WP D	Drawing in Word Processing
SS	Spreadsheet	P	Paint Document
CD	CD-ROM	Cal	Calculator

In Word check the Drawing toolbar is visible. Go to View, *click* Toolbars *and tick* Drawing.

To type

- Everything that should be typed onto the computer is highlighted, to make it easy to follow.

To draw

- Use drawing tools directly onto the page.

To use the calculator or Microsoft Paint

- Open the calculator or Microsoft Paint from the Accessories menu.

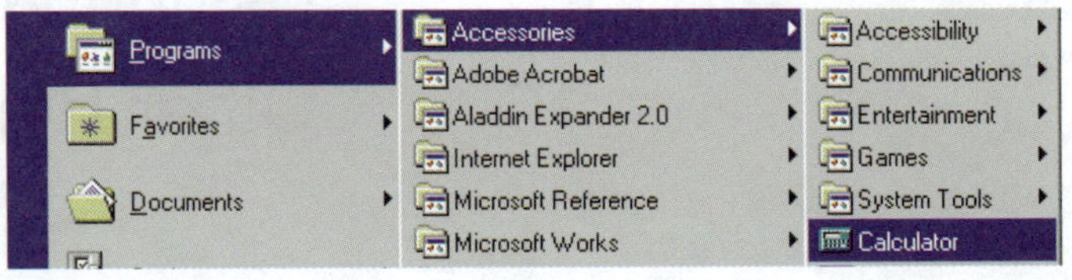

Saving

- Get into the habit of saving your work soon after starting a new document – then you will not lose it accidentally.

To save

- Click on File .
- Click on Save .
- Save in My Documents.

Each person in the family could have their own folder in My Documents.

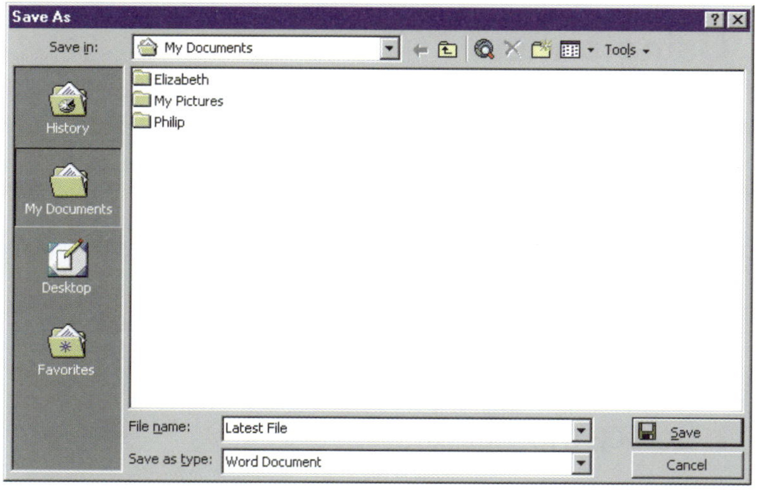

New work

- There are many ideas to try on each page.
- Start a new document for special ideas you want to keep.

Common problems

- To stop unwanted capitals appearing, click Tools , AutoCorrect... and remove ticks from Capitalize boxes.
- Insert key Insert allows you to either insert new letters or write over old ones. If OVR is showing, tap the Insert key Insert once to remove it.

Mistakes

- To undo a mistake hold Ctrl and tap Z once.

Hold Ctrl and tap Y to redo one keystroke.

Mouse speed

- You need to double-click the mouse quite fast.
- If you can't click fast enough you can slow the speed required.
- To do this, alter the mouse setting in Control Panel Mouse .

To select text

- Text must be selected and highlighted before it can be altered. To select it you can double-click on a word, triple-click on a line, or click and drag across a whole block of text.

The way a page is set out is called its format.
You can create your own formats or use ready-made formats.

Using bullets

- Make the text size 36.
- Choose a Font.
- Click ▾ and click Whole Page.
- Type People to Invite and press ↵Enter.
- Type a list of people.
- Select the heading.
- In Format choose Borders and Shading....
- Choose a border and shading you like.

- Click OK.
- Select your list.
- From More Buttons » choose Bullets ☰ to make your list stand out.

Fancy bullets

- Type Things to Eat. List them.
- Type Games to Play. List them.
- Make the headings stand out with Borders and Shading... from Format menu.
- Select the things to eat.
- From the Format menu choose Bullets and Numbering....
- In the dialogue box click one you like. Click OK.
- Select the list of games you have typed.
- From the Bullets and Numbering... menu, click Picture... and click the picture bullet you like.

Change style

- Select the titles and click Underline U, Italic I or Bold B to change the style.

Themed formats

- From Format choose Theme....
- Click on each Theme to see what it looks like.
- Choose one and click OK.
- To insert a patterned horizontal line click Borders and Shading....
- Click Horizontal Line....
- Click on the one you like.
- Use the lines to divide up your writing.

Create your own style template

- Plan your own format by opening a New Document.
- Change the font.
- Add borders, shading and bullets to add your own style to the page.
- You could use Theme..., Callouts and WordArt... to make a really wacky page.
- Click File and click Save As....
- Choose Document Template in Save as type: box.
- Create a New Folder.
- Give it a name you will remember.
- Save your template.

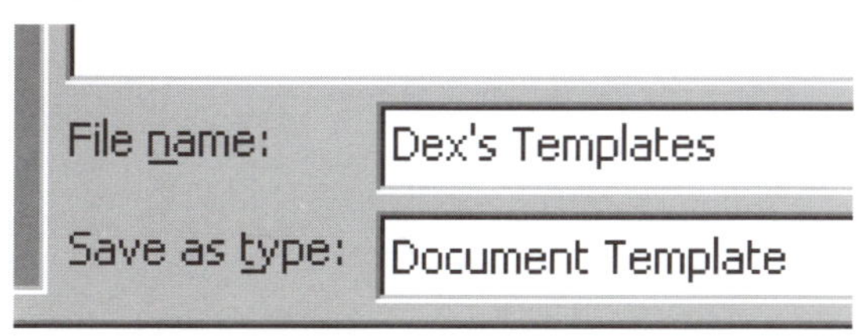

Using your template

- Open Word.
- Click File. Click New.... Click the tab for your templates.
- Double click the template to reopen and use.

Text can be made to fit all round an object.

Text wrap an advert

- Open a document in Print Layout View.
- Click and click Whole Page.
- Type FOR SALE.
- Change size of the letters to 48.
- Centre it.
- Write about what you want to sell in a slightly smaller font.
- You might, for example, want to sell your old toys.
- Click in the text where you want a picture.
- Insert some Clip Art.
- Drag the picture to the size you want.
- Click View and click Toolbars and make sure the Picture toolbar is ticked.
- From the Picture toolbar choose Text Wrap.
- Click Square or Tight.

If the Picture toolbar can't be seen. Click View and click Toolbars.

To text wrap a drawing of your own:

- Click where you want it in the text.
- Use line and shape tools to draw over the text.
- Open the Picture toolbar.
- Click Text wrap.
- Click Square or Tight.

Look how the text flows around the drawing.

Clip Art

- Use Clip Art and text wrap to put pictures into your stories.

See if you can write a story and use some of this Clip Art.

Gift tokens

- Click File and click Page Setup....
- Click Paper Size and click the Landscape box to choose landscape format for your new document.
- Click Format and click Column.
- Choose Two Columns.
- Type A TOKEN FOR YOU and your name in size 48.
- Add text explaining what you will do.
- Copy and paste the promise to fill about a column and a half, e.g. I will wash the car for you.
- Click in the text and insert a Clip Art or a drawing of your own to illustrate what you have written.
- Click on the picture.
- Click the text wrap button from the picture toolbar.
- Text wrap a shape with your name somewhere else in the text to say who it is from.
- Print the card and fold it.

A TOKEN FOR YOU

I will look after your cat every day for a week. I will look after your cat every day for a week. I will look after your cat every day for a week. I will look after your cat every day for a week. I will look after your cat every day for a week. I will look after your cat every day for a week. I will look after your cat every day for a week. I will look after your cat every day for a week. I will look after your cat every day for a week. I will look after your cat every day for a week. I will look after your cat every day for a week. I will look after your cat

every day for a week. I will look after your cat every day for a week. I will look after your cat every day for a week. I will look after your cat every day for a week. I will look after your cat every day for a week. I will look after your cat every day for a week. I will look after your cat every day for a week. I will look after your cat every day for a week. I will look after your cat every day for a week. I will look after your cat every day for a week. I will look after your cat every day for a week. I will look after your cat every day for a week. I will look after your cat every day for a week. I will look after your cat every day for a

Love from Data

Pet passport

- Type Pet Passport.
- Type the words:

  Name
  Address
  Date of birth
  Type of animal
  Distinguishing features
  Favourite food

- Text wrap a rectangle to fit to the left of the text.
- Use the Rectangle tool to frame the card.
- When the centre goes blank click Order from the Draw menu.
- Click Send Behind Text.

Save as a template so you can make copies for your friends.

- Scan a photo to fit the box or add a Clip Art picture for fun.
- Paste this in the back of a notebook.
- Make stamps to show where the pets have been.

Print the page and add a photo.

You can make your own templates.

Make a prepared outline letter

- Type your address and postcode.
- Tap ↵Enter twice.
- Select all of the writing and align to the right ≡.
- Press ↵Enter and align left ≡.
- Click Insert and click Date and Time....

Make sure the Update automatically *box* ☑ *is ticked and click* OK.

Susie Stone
Silly Street
Sandhill
S08 8S0

5/16/00

- Type Dear.
- Tap ↵Enter three or four times.
- Finish the letter with Best wishes from.
- Click File. Click Save As....
- Choose Document Template in Save as type: box.
- Open your own templates folder.
- Give it a name you will remember.
- Click Save.

When you want to write a letter click File. *Click* New... *and then open your template. Add the name of your friend and the text. The date is updated automatically.*

Make a club template

- Click File menu and click New....
- Click the template you want to open.
- You could add your club logo to the letterhead.

You cannot open templates if you click 🗋.

Computer templates

- Click File and click New....
- This opens the templates.
- Click in Other Documents and open the Calendar Wizard and make a calendar of your own.

Homework template

- Open a new document in Print Layout View.
- Click and click Whole Page.
- Click View and click Header and Footer. The Header and Footer toolbar will show up.
- In the header type:

  Homework for (type your teacher's name) from (type your name).
- Tab across the footer and click and from the Header and Footer toolbar.
- In the main part of the page type Subject Heading.
- Make this word big and bold.
- Save it as Homework template in your templates folder.

- When you need a new Homework page click File, click New... and open the homework template.

Make the document double line spaced by holding Ctrl *and tapping 2. Now you'll need less to fill a page.*

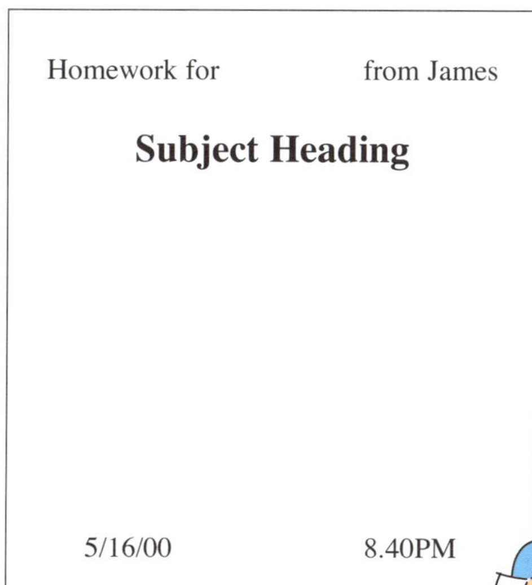

Homework for from James

Subject Heading

5/16/00 8.40PM

Letter to all your relatives and friends

- Open the template.
- After Dear leave a space.
- Write a long letter with news about your family and friends.
- Save as a new template in your templates folder. Call it 'news'.
- Open your news template.
- Type the name of a friend.
- Add a few lines to ask after their family to make it personal.
- Print, sign and send.
- Do this for each of your friends.

If you want to send the letter by email select all the letter and copy it. Paste the copy into an email.

Text, graphics and tables can be combined in different layouts.

Planning

- Plan projects on paper to get the look you need.
- First list the information you want to display.
- Then consider the best ways to do it.

pictures logo text headings tables maps what else?

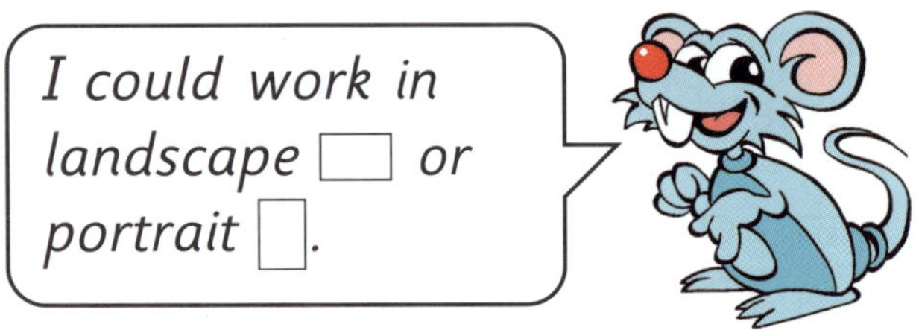

ID cards

- Try these ideas in a Word document.

  Type:

SECRET SOCIETY	(size 18)
Code name......................	(size 10)
Membership No.............	(size 10)
Password.........................	(size 10)

- Drag an oblong for the picture to the right of the text.
- Use a text box to put a label saying: add photo here in the frame.
- Add a logo.

- Drag a rectangle for a border across the text and shape.
- From Draw ▾ click Order and click Send to Back and Send Behind Text.
- Select all (Ctrl + A) and copy it (Ctrl + C).
- Paste a copy for each member of the club.

Make a poster for your door

KEEP OUT

Secret meeting in progress

Do not disturb
Members only

Please knock and give the password

Strangers beware

Newsletter

Splattermouse Strikes Back

Today we saw some amazing scenes, that made all of us who are mice very proud. A huge cat, that has been terrorising our neighbourhood for over three days, has finally been put in his place by none other than our good friend Splattermouse. Splattermouse has even managed to get the cat to agree to bring us fresh cheese every morning. This is not the first time that Splattermouse has come to our rescue. About three days ago a large frog was seen prowling round our lovely town, and it was feared he might end up squashing one of us. Splattermouse though, soon scared him off.

Documents

The Big Cheese Group

RULES

1 No cats allowed.
2 Keep whiskers clean.
3 Leave carving knives at mousehole door.

PASSWORD

Squeak twice and ask for Data.

Club stationery

The Big Cheese Group

Maps and Plans

Paint and drawing packages can be used to draw maps and plans.

Country map

- Open Paint from the Accessories menu.
- Use the Brush tool to paint a wiggly outline for a fantasy island.
- Add a river, volcano, lake and mountains.

- Use the Airbrush tool to add a swamp, woods and smoke to the volcano.
- Use the Pencil tool to add details such as trees, roads and streams.
- Use Fill with the Colour tool to flood sea area with pale colour.
- Choose another colour for the land.
- Add labels with the text tool.
- Use the line tool to add a compass showing north.

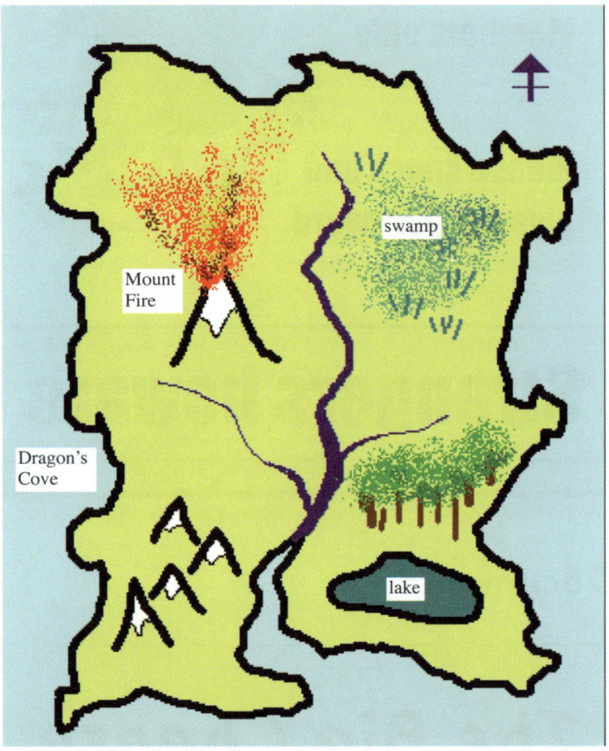

Town plan (drawing)

- Open Word.
- Use the Scribble tool to draw roads and rivers.
- Colour them with the Line Colour tool.
- Use the Freeform tool to draw woods and parks. Fill with green.
- Click to draw wider roads.
- Colour the main roads red and the minor roads brown.
- Use the shape tools to add buildings.
- Add labels with the text tool.

Make a plan of your room

- Use the Line tool [Line tool icon] to draw the outline.
- Add rectangles for windows.
- Use the Curve tool [Curve tool icon] to add the door space.
- Add rectangles to show your furniture.
- Label the furniture using text boxes.

Remember to click No Fill *and* No Line *after you have typed in the text.*

- Move the furniture round the room to redesign the layout.
- Rotate pieces by using Rotate or Flip from the Draw ▾ menu.

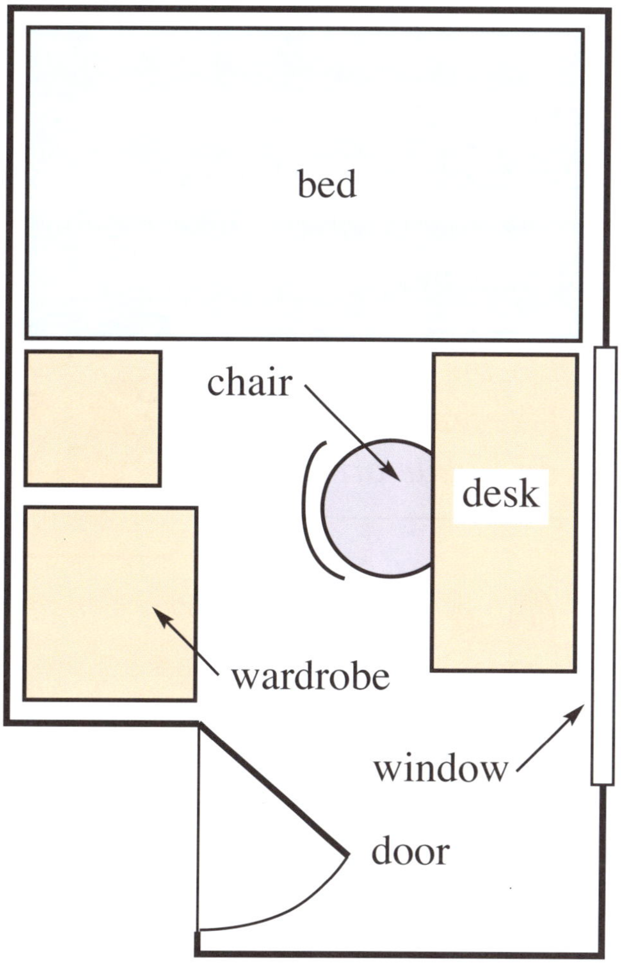

Garden design (Word)

- Use the line or rectangle tools to draw the perimeters of the house and garden.
- Group a large green circle and a small brown circle to make a tree.
- Shrink and copy to make several trees of different sizes.
- Change their sizes and add to the plan.
- Colour different shapes from AutoShapes ▾ to make flowerbeds.
- Group the parts and copy, stretch or shrink to fit the garden.
- Add seats, a pond and other features.

If the flowerbed rectangle hides the plants, click Draw ▾, Order *and* Send to Back.

Drawing Diagrams

Diagrams and charts can be drawn on the computer.

Flowcharts

- Use textboxes and drawing tools to make charts which show a sequence of activities.

Do the boxes and text first. Then add your arrows.

In AutoShapes ▾ *use* Flowchart, Basic Shapes *and* Block Arrows *to help you.*

Remember, you can make these menus float.

The diamonds are 'decision boxes' and the rectangles are 'do something' boxes.

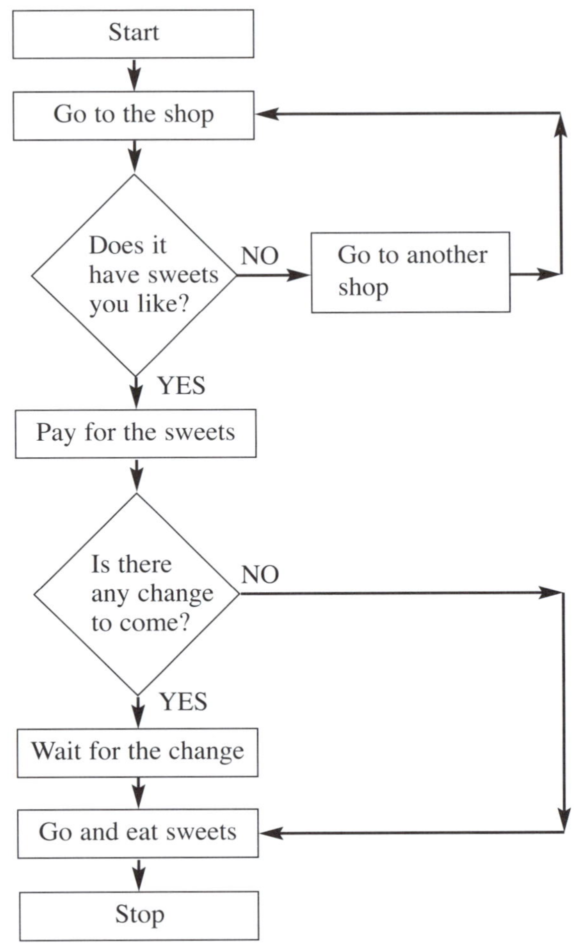

Make a flow chart to show the stages in catching mice.

Circuit diagrams

- Copy these symbols to draw circuit diagrams.

battery (1 cell)	battery (2 cells)	switch	electric bell	electric buzzer	lamp	motor

Drawing keys

- Use lines and shapes to make a sorting key.
- Make up questions to sort other animals.

Use Text Boxes and arrows to make a branching key like this.

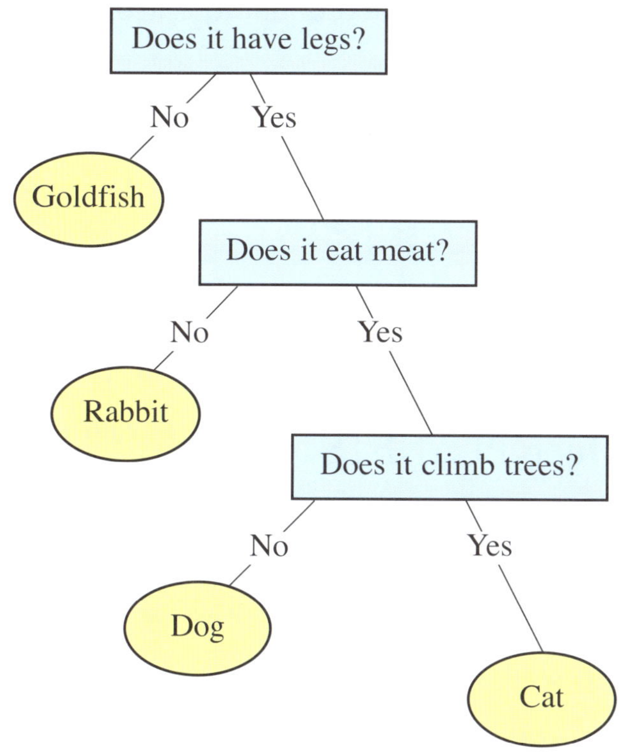

Concept maps

- Make a concept map like this for your school topics.

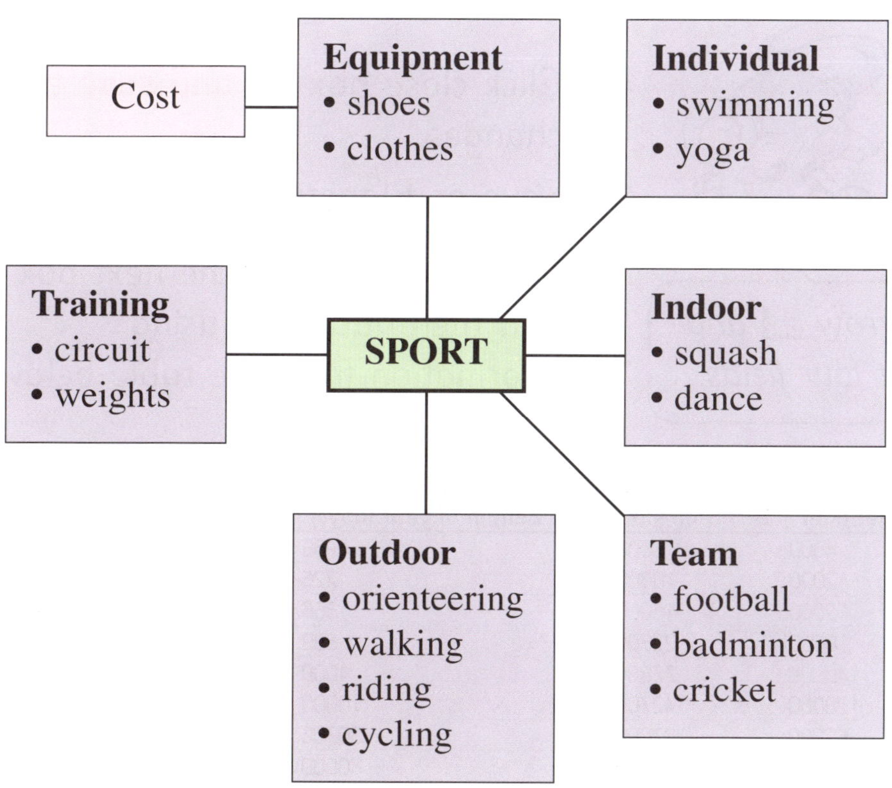

Concept maps are a good way to plan the parts of a project.

A database layout can include graphics and formatting features.
Data can be sorted using Filters.

Plan the fields

- Open Access.
- Click Blank Access database button.
- Click OK.
- Type PLANETS in the File name: box.
- Open your folder. Click Create.
- In the next box click Open.
- Type in these field names.

  Planet name
  Type
  Diameter (km)
  Distance from the sun (km)
  Length of year (days)
  Length of a day (days)

Planet Database : Table

Field Name	Data Type
Planet name	Text
Type	Text
Diameter (km)	Number
Dist from sun (km)	Number
Length of year (days)	Number
Length of day (days)	Text
	Text
	Memo
	Number

In Data Type *click the arrow and click* Number *for the last four fields.*

- Click the close button on the table.
- Click Yes.
- Give it a name and click OK.
- Click No and double-click the name of your database to open it.
- Fill the database using the information below.

Change the width of each column by dragging or double-clicking here.

- Click close box and save the changes.
- Save as Planets.
- Click No to the next box and then add data using information from the table below.

Planet Database : Table

Planet name	Type	Diameter (km)	Dist from sun (km)	Length of year (days)	Length of day (days)
Mercury	rock	4000	58000000	86	59.0
Venus	rock	12000	108000000	225	243.0
Earth	rock	12000	150000000	365	1.0
Mars	rock	6000	228000000	600	1.0
Jupiter	gas	140000	778000000	4000	0.5
Saturn	gas	120000	1427000000	10000	0.5
Uranus	gas	52000	2870000000	30700	0.7
Neptune	gas	48000	4497000000	60000	1.8
Pluto	rock	3000	5900000000	90000	6.0

Add a new field

- Click Insert and click Column.
- Double-click on the heading **Field1** to change the name of the field.
- Name the field Notes.
- Use this field to add notes about each planet.

Sort the records

- Sort the planets in order of size, the lengths of their days or years.
- Click once in the column you want to sort by.
- From Records choose Sort.
- Click Sort Ascending to see the smallest first.
- Click OK.
- Click once in another column.
- Click Sort Descending and sort that column with the biggest at the top.

Filter one field

- To see only the planets which are bigger than 12000 in diameter click Filter By Form.

To see all the records again, click Records *and click* Remove Filter/Sort.

- Type >12000 in the diameter column.
- Click Apply Filter.
- All the planets which are bigger than 12000 will be displayed.

When you type in a number, don't use spaces or commas.

Filter two fields

- To see only the planets which are smaller than Earth and further from the sun than Earth, do this:
- Click Records and click Filter.
- Click Filter By Form.
- In the diameter column type <12000.
- In the distance column type >150000000.
- Click Apply Filter/Sort to see planets smaller than Earth, but further from the sun.

Spreadsheets can check your finances.

Plan your holiday budget

- List your holiday expenses.
- Use a spreadsheet like this to calculate your budget.

	A	B	C	D
1	To buy	price	quantity	cost
2	films	3.99	4	=B2*C2
3	suntan lotion	2.45	2	
4	books	5.5	3	
5	T shirt	10.5	2	
6	hat	5.6	1	
7	shoes	2.99	2	
8			TOTAL	=SUM(D2:D7)
9			Money left to spend	=100-D8

- In cell D2 write the formula =B2*C2 to work out the total cost of the films.
- Copy the formula and paste into the cells D3 – D7 below.

Click cell D8 and click Σ. This will add up D2 to D7.

- In D9 write the formula 100 (or whatever number of pounds you have to spend) minus D8. This will take your total bills away from the money you have to spend.
- Try altering the figures to see what would happen if you bought more or less films, or bought cheaper film.

Currency conversion

- Use a spreadsheet to work out how much currency you will get for your pounds.
- Compare prices from banks, building societies and travel agents.
- In D2 write a formula to calculate the number of Euros you will get.
- Paste the formula into the cells below.
- Do another spreadsheet to convert dollars to pounds.

	A	B	C	D
1		Euros to the Pound	Number of Pounds to Convert	Total number of Euros
2	bank	1.67	75	
3	building society	1.69		
4	travel agent	1.65		
5	airport rate	1.63		

Budgeting with holiday brochures

- Use holiday brochures to find the cost of holidays you'd like to go on.
- Add £10 for each meal not provided by the hotel.
- Estimate the costs of different types of clothing and equipment for each holiday.
- Add other expenses to your spreadsheet.
- Use Auto Sum Σ to find out the totals for each holiday.
- Make graphs to compare the cost of each holiday.
- Use a word processing document to write about the holidays and paste your graphs into it.

	A	B	C	D	E	F
1	location	cost of holiday	estimated cost of food	new clothes and equipment	spending money for each trip	TOTAL
2	France (skiing holiday)					
3	Spain (beach holiday)					
4	Greece (sailing holiday)					

Hot holiday spots

	Jan	Feb	Mar	Apr	May	Jun	July	Aug	Sep	Oct	Nov	Dec
London	6	7	10	13	16	21	22	21	18	14	10	7
Orlando	22	23	25	28	31	32	32	32	31	28	24	22

- Spreadsheets can help you draw a graph of the temperature in holiday destinations.
- Use a brochure to enter the data for places you would like to go to.
- Look at the table comparing London and Florida.
- Temperatures are in °C.
- Enter the data into a spreadsheet then select the whole table.
- Click New Chart.
- Click the Line graph Line.
- Add a title to the graph.

A spreadsheet can help plan a good diet.
It can calculate and graph food values.

Cereal comparison

	A	B	C	D	E
1		Fat	Carbohydrate	Sugar	Calories
2	Weetabix				
3	Frosties				
4	Branflakes				
5	Cornflakes				

- Use the data on cereal packets to compare the fat, sugar and carbohydrate content of cereals.
- Set up a spreadsheet like the one above to show the food value of 100g of different cereals.
- Type in the names of the cereals that you eat.
- Type in the food value in the correct column. (The data is on the side of the packet.)
- Drag across all the cells to select them.
- Click Chart and make charts to compare the food values.
- Paste your graphs into your word processing writing.

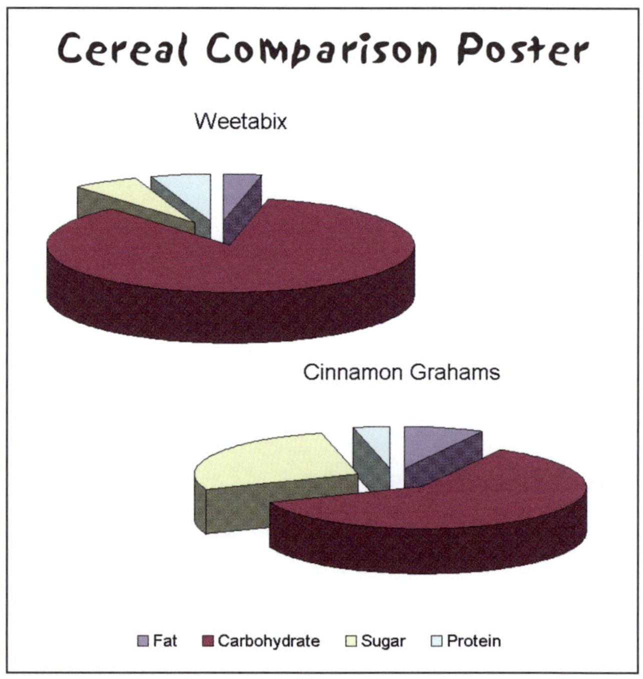

Other food

- Use a spreadsheet table and graphs to compare other foods such as tins of beans, yoghurts and ready-cooked meals.

Bean brand	Calories	Added sugar	Salt	Fat

Milk

- Make a spreadsheet which compares the food value of different types of milk.

	Calories per100g	Fat in gm	Protein in gm
Full cream milk	65	4	3
Semi-skimmed	45	2	3.2
Skimmed	33	0.1	3.4
Evaporated	160	9	8.6
Condensed	320	9	8.3
Double cream	450	48	1.5

- Make some graphs to compare types of milk.

Calorie counting with a spreadsheet

- Use the information on this page to choose your food for one day.
- Most eleven-year-old children need about 2200 calories.

Don't forget to include snacks and drinks!

- Put these headings in row 1.

Food
Calories
Number of helpings
Calorie total

- List the foods you want to eat in column A.
- List their food values in calories in column B.
- List the number of helpings you want in column C.
- In cell D2 put the formula =B2*C2.
- This will work out the number of calories for each food, e.g. 2 apples @ 70 calories should show 140.
- Select cell D2. Click Copy.
- Paste this formula into the cells in column D.

Type Total here.

Put the formula for adding all of column D into this cell. This shows the total calories you would eat in a day.

- See what happens if you eat lots of peanuts and cola.
- How can you eat more food but not break a 2200 calorie target?

Finding Out About France

Many different types of information can be found on CD-ROMs and the Web.

Encarta

- Open Encarta.
- On the home page click Features.
- Click InterActivities Ctrl + I.
- Click World Languages.
- Click Phrases.
- Choose French from the list of languages and listen to different phrases.
- Use the white arrow keys to get to the Home page.

France

- Type France in the Find box.
- Tap ↵Enter.
- Use the arrows to scroll across the pictures at the top of the screen.
- Name two mountain ranges in France.

1 ______________________________

2 ______________________________

- Click the sound icons to hear the music.

Soccer

- Click yearbook update to find out how France won their first world cup title in soccer.

French students

- Use the quick facts box to answer these questions.

  1 Name the French national anthem.

  ____

  2 What is the highest point in France?

  ____

  3 What are the three largest cities?

  ____

  4 What is the French currency called?

  ____

- Log on to the Yahooligans Web site http://www.yahooligans.com/

- Click **Around the World** Countries, Food, Holidays...
- Click • **Countries**
- Click • **France**
- Look at the videos of places in France.
- Meet three French students.
- See live panoramic pictures from Paris.
- Try ZipZap France in French and English. This is a tour of France for children in both languages.

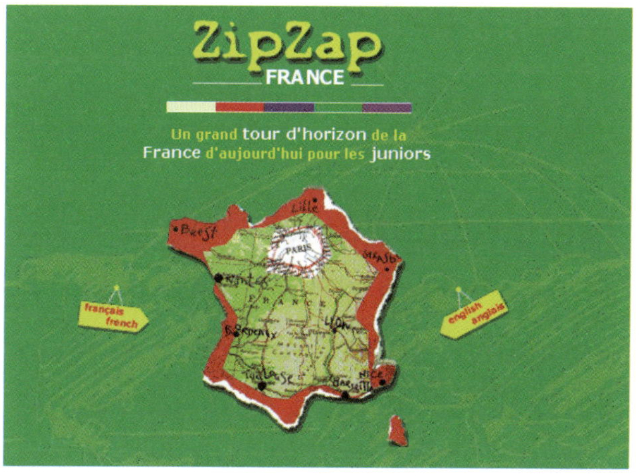

- Use the find box to discover more about places you know in France, French food and sports.

There are many different things to do on the Internet.
Type Internet addresses carefully.

Get homework help

- There are several homework Web sites where you can get help on many subjects. Teachers there will help answer questions and research questions.
- Open Yahooligans!
  http://www.yahooligans.com/
- Click on the Homework answers link in the School Bell section.

Play on-line games

- Games sites will tell you about new computer games on the market and sometimes let you play demos of these games. Some can be downloaded and kept.
- Games Domain
  http://www.gamesdomain.com/
- Gamespot
  http://www.gamespot.com/
- The Electric Playground
  http://www.elecplay.com/
- Illusionworks
  http://www.illusionworks.com/

Type the name of your favourite computer game company into a find box and see what their site looks like.

Puzzles

- Brain Teasers
  http://www.eduplace.com/math/brain/
  This site has new puzzles each week.

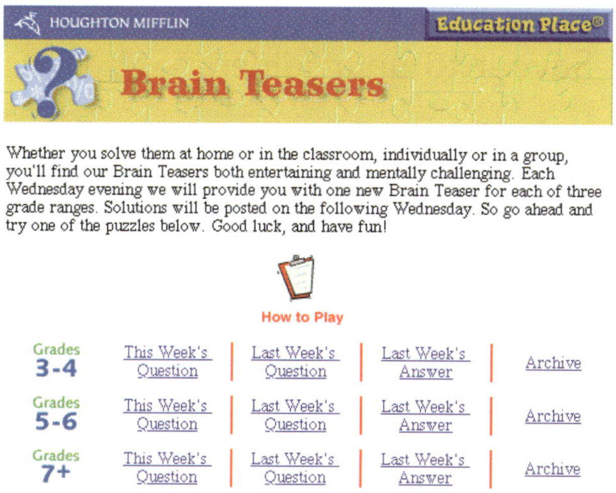

- Family Games
  http://www.familygames.com/index.html
  This site has a good selection for the whole family to enjoy.

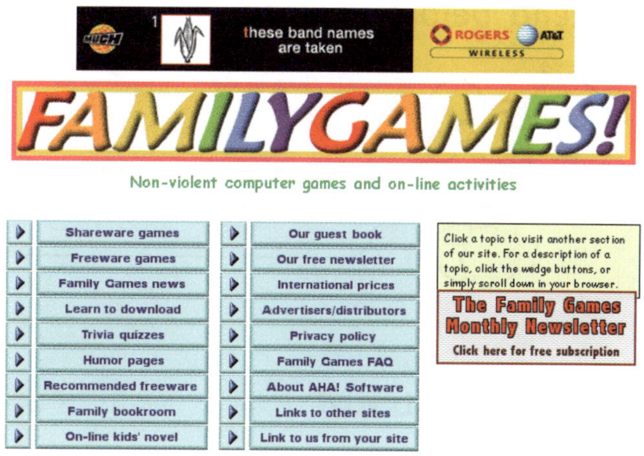

Put your work on the web

- Kids' Space
  http://www.kids-space.org/

This site has a gallery for displaying your art work, a storybook area for publishing your stories and a Beanstalk project where you can share in creating an on-line picture book. You can send sound files here as well. A guide bear will help you sort out Internet problems.

- Copy anything you want to send and paste it into an email document. You could also send it as an attachment to an email.
- A similar site is:

Kidscom
http://www.kidscom.com/

Email is a quick, cheap way to send messages.

Send a letter

- Use Word to write a message to a friend before you log on.

- Copy it.
- Save it to your folder.
- Log on.
- Click New Message and type your friend's email address.
- Paste your message. Click Send.

Send a postcard

- Log on.
- Type: http://postcards.www.media.mit.edu/Postcards/
- This takes you to the Electric postcard website.
- Choose a picture, write a message and send it.
- Your friend will get an email telling them they have a message and how to get it.

The Electric Postcard

To **send** a postcard go to the Postcard Rack.

To **pick up** a postcard go to the Pick-up Window.

The Postcard Rack has a wide variety of postcards for you to choose from. You pick the card you like, write your message, and send it off. The recipient will be notified by email that a card has been sent and to claim it at the Pick-up Window.

Cards are held at the Pick-up Window for two weeks after they are sent. In addition, they are held for two weeks after they are claimed (if they are viewed additional times, they are held longer).

It's free! There is no charge to send or receive these cards.

- You can save your postcards
- Some known browser eccentricities
- How to put links and pictures into your message
- Making a test message
- Sending multiple cards

Check our References - and visit some of our Branch Offices at other sites.
The source code and documentation are now available.

***Millions and millions** of cards have been sent!!*

New! Looking for a new way to chat with your friends? Try Chat Circles!

Greetings cards

- Other cards for birthdays, valentines and many more can be found at:

  Awesome Cyber Cards
  http://www.awesomecards.com

Find an epal

- This is like having a pen friend but you send messages by email instead of the post.
- If you don't have one, log on to a site where you can reply to an ad left by someone or leave an ad for the sort of epal you'd like. (See warning/safety note on page 32.)
- Try these sites:

  Freezone
  http://www.freezone.com/epls

  Cyberkids
  http://www.cyberkids.com/

Collaborative story

- Write a story with your epal. Take it in turns to write a section and send it.
- Try to leave the story at an exciting point for your epal to carry on. This can be much more fun and challenging than writing a whole story yourself.

Jokes and puzzles

- Send a joke or a puzzle to a friend.
- If you don't know any good ones try these sites:

  Joke Zone
  http://www.owl.on.ca/owl/joke.html

  Puzzles
  http://www.eduplace.com/math/brain/

Create a signature

- Design a signature for yourself to end your messages.

```
^    ^          8&8&            C
@ @          &8&8&8&8&          U
 ..          8&       8&        B4
(-----)      (  @   @  )        2
              \   ..   /        long
               \      /
                  O
```

Invent your own world.

Alien world

- Use a paint program to map an alien world.
- Make a key to identify forests, volcanoes, rivers, swamps, mountains and lakes.

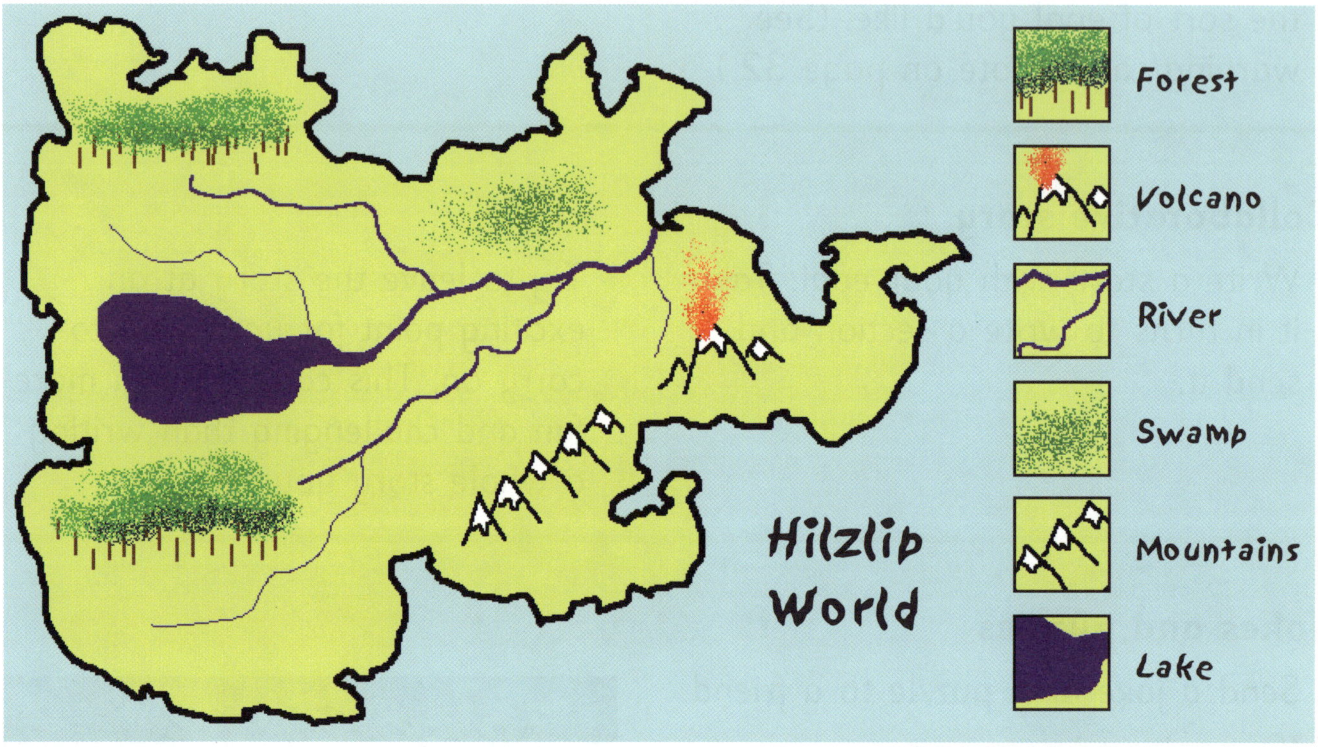

Life forms

- Use a paint program to draw a picture of each life form.
- Save to a New Folder with all other details of your world.

Alien database

- Use a database to describe the features of each life form.
- Each record should show:

  name
  size
  eating habits
  how it moves
  number of legs
  notes on special features

- Add a copy of the picture of each creature to its record card.
- Print the cards and make them into a book.

Alien transporters

- Use a drawing program to make plans of the types of transport used on the planet.
- Label the special features.

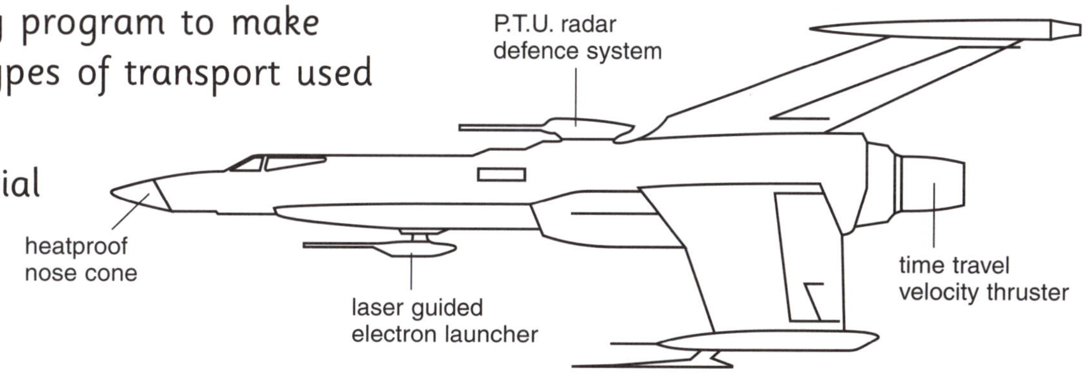

Planet map

- Use a word processing program to make a guide to the planet.
- Copy maps, plans and pictures from work saved in your planet folder.
- Use text wrap to embed them into the text.

Email

- Use email to share the writing of a story about the planet.
- Take it in turns to write a paragraph or chapter.
- Use the spellchecker to check your work before you print.
- Use the word counter to make sure you both write the same amount each time.

align
to alter the way the lines are arranged on the page.

backspace
tap this key [Backspace] to rub out mistakes (called Delete key on some machines).

CD-ROM
a Read Only Memory disc which stores information. It can hold text, graphics, sound and film clips. A CD-ROM may store games or act as an encyclopedia.

cells
boxes in a spreadsheet.

data
information stored in a database or spreadsheet.

document
a piece of work.

drag
to move something across the screen while pressing on the mouse.

draw
to start a drawing:

– open a word processing document

– open the drawing toolbar.

field
a place in a database to store information.

filter
a way of sorting information on a spreadsheet.

folder
a place to keep your documents.

font
a style of text.

footer
section at the bottom of the page which will put the same information onto each page of a document. It cannot be given columns.

format
the way text, tables and graphics are set out on a page.

formula
instructions written in a cell which make the cell do a sum. Formulas start with an equals sign.

graph
a way to show numbers as a picture.

graphic
pictures or diagrams.

group
makes separate lines and shapes into one picture which can then be moved and altered as one item.
To group:

– hold [Shift] and click the items you want to group.

– in the [Draw] menu click [Group].

handles
black squares around a shape.

header
section at the top of the page which will put the same information onto each page of a document. It cannot be given columns.

- **highlight**
  to select text or a graphic by clicking it, or dragging across it, with the mouse.
- **icon**
  a picture you click on to make the computer do a job.
- **minimize**
  reduces the page to a title bar while you do something else.
- **replace** (in the edit menu)
  will change a word throughout the document.
- **restore**
  brings back a document which has been minimized.
- **select**
  to highlight text or a graphic by clicking it, or dragging across it with the mouse.
- **spellchecker**
  checks the spellings in a document and suggests alternatives.
- **spreadsheet**
  a place to store information in a grid of cells.
- **tab**
  a marker you can use to position text or graphics.
  – tap [Tab] to move a line in steps across the page
  – drag the tab lines if you want to move a whole block of text.
- **table**
  a grid which can store information in rows and columns.
- **task wizard**
  a programme which helps to simplify complicated tasks.
- **text box**
  a block of text you can drag with a mouse.
- **text wrap**
  a way of making text flow all round a graphic without leaving any space.
- **thesaurus**
  can suggest new words with similar meanings.
- **undo**
  if you have made a mistake hold [Ctrl] and tap Z.
- **view**
  alter the way you view a page in the View menu.
  – page layout shows the margins, header and footer.
  – normal shows only the text and graphics, but not how they will print.
- **web**
  an international system of computers linked by phones.
- **window**
  a part of the screen with a frame round it.
- **zoom**
  click the icon to enlarge or shrink the display.

What is email?

- Email means electronic mail.
- It is a way of sending letters using the Internet. It is a fast, cheap way to send a message.
- Each email user has a special address.
- It looks something like this: Fred@links.co.uk
- Fred is the 'user name'. Each user can choose their own.
- @ means 'at'.
- links is the host name of the company which stores the email.
- uk is the country code.
- You need a password as well.
- Your Internet Service Provider gives you an email address.
- You may choose your user name and password.

To send an email

1. Log on by clicking on your ISP icon on the screen.
2. Open a new email document.
3. In the header type the email address of the person it will go to. (It is very important to get every detail of this right.)
4. On the subject line put a brief description of the message, e.g. Hello or Message.
5. Type the message.
6. Click the Send button.
7. Log off.

- It may take minutes or a few hours to get there but it will beat the post.
- Note: It is expensive to stay online for a long time, so try to write letters offline and then paste them into your email documents.
- Read your messages offline as well if they are long.

To reply to a message

1. Open the message.
2. Tap the Reply button. This will give you a new document with the address of the person you are writing to already in place.
3. Type your message and tap Send.

Warning

- Anyone can send you an email message. If you don't know them you don't have to reply.
- If you get a message which upsets you tell an adult.
- Don't give information about yourself to anyone you don't know in real-life, such as your home address, phone number or when you go on holiday.